Serving

Tim May

with illustrations by
Taffy

Series Editor: James Jones

◆》》The Bible Reading Fellowship

1

Brought up to go to church, Ann's faith in God grew slowly. Then a two-week Christian campaign, 'God Cares', changed everything. Suddenly God became real to her, and Ann realized she wanted to serve him.

For a while she had been aware of the needs of the Third World. She wanted to do something to put God's love into action. So she offered to God her training as a nurse, and found herself working in a hospital near Madras, India.

God became real in Ann's life, and he called her to serve him—just like Jesus called Simon:

 **Read Luke 5:3–11**

Jesus ... said to Simon, 'Push the boat out ... and ... let down your nets for a catch.'

'Master,' Simon answered, 'we worked hard all night long and caught nothing. But if you say so, I will let down the nets.' They let them down and caught such a large number of fish that the nets were about to break ... When Simon Peter saw what had happened, he fell on his knees before Jesus and said, 'Go away from me, Lord! I am a sinful man!'

... Jesus said to Simon, 'Don't be afraid; from now on you will be catching people.'

They pulled the boats up on the beach, left everything, and followed Jesus.

Jesus called both Ann and Simon ... and in their different ways they served him.

Today, he's calling you. It might not be to India. It could be on the estate where you live. But he's calling you. He wants you to serve him. How will you respond?

Look at the sentence below, then mark on the 1–10 scale how much it applies to you:

I want to serve Jesus.

1   2   3   4   5   6   7   8   9   10

Dear Jesus, thank you for your call. Thank you that you want me to serve you. Please show me what you want me to do. And give me the strength to do it. Amen.

Follow me

You're the one!

It was a dream come true. Mark had supported United all his life. Now he had signed schoolboy forms, and was walking through the players' gate for the first time.

Then his heart sank. He was led into a room, where his first job was to clean the first team boots.

For a while, it was a big anti-climax. But then he realized whose boots he was cleaning: his hero—the United and England centre-forward, whose goals he'd cheered so often.

Suddenly the task wasn't so bad. In fact, he gave it all he'd got. And as he rubbed the polish in, he willed the boots to score the winning goal on Saturday.

Here's the moment when Simon Peter realized he was serving someone special:

 Read Matthew 16:13–16

Jesus . . . asked his disciples, 'Who do people say the Son of Man is?'

'Some say John the Baptist,' they answered. 'Others say Elijah, while others say Jeremiah or some other prophet.'

'What about you?' he asked them. 'Who do you say I am?'

Simon Peter answered, 'You are the Messiah, the Son of the living God.'

Mark suddenly realized whose boots he was polishing: the England centre forward . . . his hero.

Simon Peter suddenly realized who it was who had called him to serve him. Jesus was none other than *the Son of the living God.*

The same Jesus is calling you. And if, like Mark, you ever have second thoughts, remember who you're serving: not the local centre forward . . . but the King and Lord of all.

In the word square are ten words that people have used to describe Jesus. Find them all, then tick the one which, for you, best says who Jesus is:

```
R B D N E I R F
U P E H P C H L
O R W L R A D O
I O G N I K O R
V P K S E J G D
A H S G S N A B
S E Z C T V X H
M T N A V R E S
```

King
Prophet
Elijah
Friend
Lord
God
Servant
Messiah
Priest
Saviour

*Dear Jesus, Lord and God, King and
Friend: when serving you gets
difficult, help me to remember who
I'm serving. Amen.*

Sharon looked in the mirror, and hated herself. Yet another zit. Why couldn't she look like that Andrea in her class? All the boys fancied her. But no one ever asked Sharon out.

Then the letter-box flapped. To her amazement Sharon found that one of the letters was for her. It was in a pink envelope too, and perfumed.

Sharon ran upstairs, her heart pounding. She ripped open the envelope, and couldn't believe her eyes: 'I love you. Be my Valentine.'

Sharon looked into the mirror again. This time she saw herself in a new light. Someone loved her! Maybe she wasn't so bad looking after all.

What happened to Sharon gave her a new way of looking at herself. The same thing happened to Simon when he met Jesus:

 Read John 1:41–42

At once [Andrew] found his brother Simon and told him, 'We have found the Messiah.' (This word means 'Christ'.) Then he took Simon to Jesus.

Jesus looked at him and said, 'Your name is Simon son of John, but you will be called Cephas.' (This is the same as Peter and means 'a rock'.)

Jesus gave Simon a new name. He could see things in Simon that marked him out as a great leader. Those gifts made him an ideal foundation stone for the Church. So Jesus called him Peter—which means 'a rock'.

Sharon got a new name when the postman arrived. Before, she called herself 'ugly'. The Valentine called her 'beautiful'.

Jesus gives all his servants a new name. If you have called yourself 'forgotten', Jesus wants to call you 'remembered'. If you have called yourself 'worthless', Jesus wants to call you 'precious'. If you have called yourself 'useless', Jesus wants to call you 'of service'.

Link each old name to its opposite new name:

Ugly	**Welcome**
Forgotten	**New Beginning**
Worthless	**Remembered**
Useless	**Beautiful**
Rejected	**Of service**
Failure	**Loved**
Unwanted	**Precious**

Dear Jesus, thank you that you give your servants a new name. Thank you that no one is 'useless' to you. Help me to believe it, and to play my part in serving you. Amen.

The new name

Jesus had only hours left. Very soon he would be arrested, tortured and executed.

He called his friends together. He wanted to give them a way of remembering him. So he tore a loaf apart, saying it was like his body. He poured out wine, saying it was like his blood. He told his followers to 'do this in memory of me'.

Then he turned to Simon Peter:

 *Read Luke 22:31–34*

'Simon, Simon! Listen! Satan has received permission to test all of you, to separate the good from the bad, as a farmer separates the wheat from the chaff. But I have prayed for you, Simon, that your faith will not fail. And when you turn back to me, you must strengthen your brothers.'

Peter answered, 'Lord, I am ready to go to prison with you and to die with you!'

'I tell you, Peter,' Jesus said, 'the cock will not crow tonight until you have said three times that you do not know me.'

Pray for me, Jesus

Jesus knew that his servant, Peter, would let him down when the crunch came. He knew that, however full of brave words in private, Peter would bottle out in public when Jesus was arrested.

But even though he knows that Peter will let him down, Jesus still prays for him: *I have prayed for you, Peter . . .*

Jesus prayed for Peter and, as we shall see, his prayer was heard. Today, the Bible says (Romans 8:34), he is praying for us. So when you're serving him and things get difficult, remember: Jesus is praying for you. And even if you trip up from time to time, he'll strengthen you to go on.

Here's a list of ways in which you could serve Jesus. Choose one of them, and then ask Jesus to pray for you:

☐ Offer to read the Bible in church.
☐ Do a car wash for Christian Aid.
☐ Visit someone in an old people's home.
☐ Deliver Christmas or Easter cards for your church.
☐ Offer to help in your local Oxfam shop.
☐ Help to take a service in a local hospital.
☐ Shopping or gardening for someone housebound.
☐ Offer to make coffee after the service.

Dear Jesus, thank you that you prayed for Peter. Thank you that you're praying for me. As I step out and serve you, I need your prayers. Help me to remember that you're praying for me. Amen.

Just as Jesus had predicted, they came for him. Just as Jesus had predicted, it was Judas who gave him away—for a bag of silver coins. Just as Jesus had predicted, his friends all ran away and left him to it.

Then Peter had second thoughts. He followed Jesus at a distance. He found out that Jesus was on trial in the High Priest's house. He pulled up his collar and joined the others standing round a fire outside.

But try as he might to fade into the background, they recognized him. One after another, they asked him if he knew Jesus. Once, twice, he denied it, then:

 **Read Luke 22:59–62**

... another man insisted strongly, 'There isn't any doubt that this man was with Jesus, because he also is a Galilean!'

But Peter answered, 'Man, I don't know what you are talking about!'

At once, while he was still speaking, a cock crowed. The Lord turned round and looked straight at Peter, and Peter remembered that the Lord had said to him, 'Before the cock crows tonight, you will say three times that you do not know me.' Peter went out and wept bitterly.

From time to time, as servants of Jesus, we all fail. We blow our top and snap unfairly at someone. We tell lies to cover our tracks. We join in with the crowd, and pretend we don't know Jesus.

When we fail, it's important to know it's not the end of the story. For it's comforting to know that even Saint Peter failed ... very badly. Time and again they asked him if he knew Jesus. Time and again he denied it ... until the cock crew, and he knew he had failed.

Like Peter, we all fail from time to time. Score yourself out of 10 for each of the following:

I sometimes blow my top unfairly.

1 2 3 4 5 6 7 8 9 10

I sometimes tell lies to cover myself.

1 2 3 4 5 6 7 8 9 10

I sometimes pretend I don't know Jesus.

1 2 3 4 5 6 7 8 9 10

I sometimes wish there were no poor or starving people.

1 2 3 4 5 6 7 8 9 10

Sometimes I steal things, and tell myself it's all right.

1 2 3 4 5 6 7 8 9 10

cock-a-doodle do!!!

Dear Jesus, you know me, warts and all. You know I'm far from perfect. You know I often fail you. I'm sorry for the times I let you down. Please forgive me. And never give up on me. Amen.

I don't know him!

'But it's Fiona's turn to wash up!' stormed Gareth. He was just about to slam the kitchen door when his Mum called him back. 'Gareth! Fiona's exams start tomorrow. Please wash up!'

Wearily, he set to. He washed up all right, but wanted the whole world to know. Upstairs in her bedroom, cramming her biology, Fiona heard every plate and spoon thump moodily onto the draining board.

You might have been served by someone like Gareth. Someone who wants to let you know they'd rather not be serving you.

You may have served someone else like Gareth served Fiona: through gritted teeth.

That's not the way with the servant of Jesus. Our aim is to be enthusiastic . . . big hearted . . . like Peter:

 Read John 21:4–8

As the sun was rising, Jesus stood at the water's edge, but the disciples did not know that it was Jesus. Then he asked them, 'Young men, haven't you caught anything?'

'Not a thing,' they answered.

He said to them, 'Throw your net out on the right side of the boat, and you will catch some.' So they threw the net out and could not pull it back in, because they had caught so many fish.

The disciple whom Jesus loved said to Peter, 'It is the Lord!' When Peter heard that it was the Lord, he wrapped his outer garment round him (for he had taken his clothes off) and jumped into the water. The other disciples came to shore in the boat, pulling the net full of fish.

Dear Jesus, Peter was a big-hearted enthusiast. May I serve other people in his generous, whole-hearted way. Amen.

I love this bit about Peter! He's on a boat, fishing, in the middle of the lake. He suddenly realizes Jesus is at the water's edge. So he gets dressed . . . and then jumps into the water! Meanwhile the other (sensible) ones come in the boat.

But forget the sensible ones for now. Keep in mind the picture of Peter. He's so enthusiastic for Jesus that he gets dressed and then leaps into the water.

Aim to serve Jesus in that same crazy, big-hearted, generous way. You won't go far wrong.

On the line, write one way in which you've served Jesus recently:

. . . .

Now imagine the bar below is a thermometer. Shade it in to the extent that you were enthusiastic—big hearted——in your service.

IN AT THE
DEEP
E N D

7 The second chance

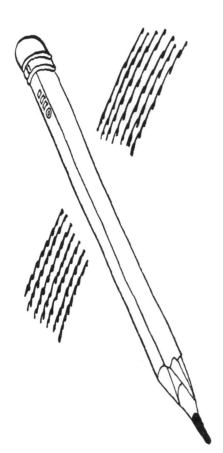

'Nicola! How could you?' The youth leader's voice quavered with disbelief. 'We trusted you!'

Nicola's youth club were planning a trip to Alton Towers. They'd opened a bank account to save up for it, and given Nicola the job of locking away the money. Then someone had seen her stealing it, slipping a roll of fivers into her back pocket.

At Nicola's club a small committee of members made the decisions. The youth leader asked the group to decide what to do about Nicola.

She couldn't believe their decision. 'We don't want the police involved,' they said. 'We want to give Nicola a second chance. Everyone knows what she's done. We don't think she'd do it again.'

Imagine how Nicola felt, to be given a second chance. That's just what Jesus did for Peter. Remember Peter let him down, standing by the fire? This is what happens when they meet again:

THE SECOND CHANCE

Read John 21:15–17

... *Jesus said to Simon Peter, 'Simon son of John, do you love me more than these others do?'*

'Yes, Lord,' he answered, 'you know that I love you.'

Jesus said to him, 'Take care of my lambs.' A second time Jesus said to him, 'Simon son of John, do you love me?'

'Yes, Lord,' he answered, 'you know that I love you.'

Jesus said to him, 'Take care of my sheep.' A third time Jesus said, 'Simon, son of John, do you love me?'

Peter ... said to him, 'Lord, you know everything; you know that I love you!'

Jesus said to him, 'Take care of my sheep.'

Jesus gave Peter a second chance. Three times he'd said he didn't know Jesus. Now, three times, Jesus gives Peter a chance to express his love for him.

More than that, he gives Peter a job: *Take care of my lambs—look after my people.*

See? When Peter let Jesus down it wasn't the end of the story. Jesus helped Peter to begin again ... and even gave him a key job in the Church.

In the box, jot down lightly in pencil some ways in which you've let Jesus down:

Now pray:

Dear Jesus, I'm sorry for every time I've let you down. Like Peter, please give me a second chance. Please forgive me and help me to begin again.

Now rub out what you wrote in the box. Jesus has given you a new start!

Three years ago, Eileen was given three years to live. She had myeloma, a form of cancer which affects her bone marrow and her blood.

One of the first things Eileen did was to ask her church to pray for her. The knowledge that people were praying for her was a powerful thing . . .

'The chemotherapy was horrible,' she remembers. 'But as I lay in hospital, all I could think about were the people at church. Their prayers were like a warm, comforting cloak . . . it was so uplifting.'

Praying for sick people is an important part of serving Jesus. That's why you'll find Peter doing just that:

Read Acts 3:1–8

> *One day Peter and John went to the Temple . . . There at the Beautiful Gate . . . was a man who had been lame all his life . . . When he saw Peter and John going in, he begged them to give him something. They looked straight at him, and Peter said, 'Look at us!' So he looked at them, expecting to get something from them. But Peter said to him, 'I have no money at all, but I give you what I have: in the name of Jesus Christ of Nazareth I order you to get up and walk!' Then he took him by his right hand and helped him up. At once the man's feet and ankles became strong; he jumped up, stood on his feet, and started walking around.*

As Peter found, it costs nothing to pray for poorly people. And as Eileen found, the rewards are deep and rich—better than money.

More than that, it doesn't matter how old or young you are: you can still pray for the sick. As Eileen herself put it, 'There is no age limit on voices praying for sick people. No matter how young the voice . . . your prayer will still be heard.'

So have a think. Who do you know who is poorly? Write their names in the box:

```
┌─────────────────────────────┐
│                             │
│                             │
│                             │
└─────────────────────────────┘
```

Now begin to pray for those people . . . every day if you can. And if you can find a way to let them know you're praying, so much the better.

Dear Jesus, thank you that through your power, Peter and John healed the lame man. Help me as I pray for the sick. Help me to pray, believing your power to heal. Amen.

Better than money

9

The speaker droned on and on and on. He was talking about 'saints', but the little boy on the front row had long since switched off. He picked his nose. He hummed to himself. He kicked his feet on the floor.

Suddenly, the speaker had had enough. 'You boy!' he roared. 'What's a saint?' The boy was terrified, and as he looked desperately around the church, he spotted a stained glass window: 'A saint is . . . a person the light shines through!'

It's not a bad definition! Serving Jesus is all about letting his light shine through us, so that people know we're his companions.

 **Read Acts 4:8–13**

Peter, full of the Holy Spirit, answered them, 'Leaders of the people . . . if we are being questioned today about the good deed done to the lame man and how he was healed, then you should all know . . . that this man stands here before you completely well through the power of the name of Jesus Christ of Nazareth—whom you crucified and whom God raised from death . . . The members of the Council were amazed to see how bold Peter and John were and to learn that they were ordinary men of no education. They realized then that they had been companions of Jesus.

Compani

Peter and John were *ordinary men of no education.* But they made a huge impact. The light of Jesus shone through them. Being his companions made a difference to them, as even their opponents admitted.

As with Peter, so with us. We're to be companions of Jesus. We're to show that we're his friends by letting his light shine through us.

Dear Jesus, shine through me the light of your . . . . ; may people know that I am your companion. Amen.

Put each of the following into the 'light' column or the 'darkness' column:

LIGHT	DARKNESS

Kindness
Poverty
Lies
Justice
Encouragement
Selfishness
Caring
Hate
Forgiveness
Jealousy

Now choose one word from the 'light' column and write it into the space in the prayer:

'Come on, Dad! Don't give up! We've got to find it!'

Laura was heartbroken. She'd lost her ring on the beach. Her grandma had given it to her weeks before she died.

Laura and her father had trudged up and down the beach for two hours. It was getting dark. Dad was all for going home. But Laura was determined . . .

'Please, Dad. Just ten more minutes. We might find it!'

Suddenly, a whoop of joy. There, trodden into the sand so you could hardly see it, was Laura's ring.

Hope is a very powerful thing. The hope that she might find her ring kept Laura going when Dad wanted to give up. The servant of Jesus has a living hope to keep her going when things get tough:

Read 1 Peter 1:3–5

Let us give thanks to the God and Father of our Lord Jesus Christ! Because of his great mercy he gave us new life by raising Jesus Christ from death. This fills us with a living hope, and so we look forward to possessing the rich blessings that God keeps for his people. He keeps them for you in heaven, where they cannot decay or spoil or fade away. They are for you, who through faith are kept safe by God's power for the salvation which is ready to be revealed at the end of time.

Sometimes it's hard to hope. The world often looks a very dark place. Sometimes it looks as though the good people will be swept away by the bad.

But God has raised Jesus from the dead. He shows us that our destination is glory. We have a living hope to keep us going when things get tough.

What things do you hope for? Write them in the box below:

Now underline which of those things you believe God can give you. Then pray:

Dear God, please keep my hope alive. When evil looks poised to sweep away good, help me to trust that you're in control. Amen.

I've found it !!!

Living for Jesus

Sidney had been a fool. He'd bought an Airfix Vulcan bomber, but thrown away the instructions. After all . . . he'd been modelling for years. He didn't need instructions.

Now he wished he'd followed them. The wings were on back to front. The tailplane stuck out from the bottom of the aircraft. And he had one part he couldn't fit in . . . the little plastic pilot, in sitting position, complete with life-jacket.

Clear, simple guidelines are there to help us. They help us do something step by step, so we don't take a wrong turning on the way.

Here's a set of step-by-step guidelines from Peter. He offers them to anyone who is serving Jesus:

 Read 2 Peter 1:5–8

> . . . *do your best to add goodness to your faith; to your goodness add knowledge; to your knowledge add self-control; to your self-control add endurance; to your endurance add godliness; to your godliness add Christian affection; and to your Christian affection add love. These are the qualities you need, and if you have them in abundance, they will make you active and effective in your knowledge of our Lord Jesus Christ.*

Each of the following statements is based on one of the eight qualities Peter mentioned. Score yourself out of 10 for each one, for how much it applies to you:

I am a kind person.

1   2   3   4   5   6   7   8   9   10

I believe in God.

1   2   3   4   5   6   7   8   9   10

I want to get to know the Bible better.

1   2   3   4   5   6   7   8   9   10

When I'm tempted to lose my temper I can control that impulse.

1   2   3   4   5   6   7   8   9   10

I can stick at tasks, even when they get difficult.

1   2   3   4   5   6   7   8   9   10

I love God.

1   2   3   4   5   6   7   8   9   10

I do my best to like the people around me.

1   2   3   4   5   6   7   8   9   10

I want to show the love of Jesus in action.

1   2   3   4   5   6   7   8   9   10

Now take your lowest score. What one thing could you do to make it higher? Write it in this space:

....

....

Dear Jesus, thank you for Peter's guidelines. Help me to base my life on them. May I be 'active and effective' for you. Amen.

Michael was in the Scouts at his church. For one of his awards, he did some community service in an old people's home.

There, he struck up a friendship with Alice. He'd empty her bins, get bits of shopping, and often stay on to keep her company.

One of Alice's pet hates was 'religion'. 'They're all hypocrites!' she'd snort. 'All of them!' Michael said nothing.

One day Michael's church went on a ramble. The local paper saw them off, and there was Michael in the picture, along with the others.

Alice saw the picture. Next time Michael came she asked him about it: 'Do you go to church?' Michael said he did. The word 'hypocrite' never passed Alice's lips again.

Servants of Jesus blaze the trail for Jesus—like John the Baptist did:

 **Read Mark 1:4–8**

John appeared in the desert, baptizing and preaching. 'Turn away from your sins and be baptized,' he told the people, 'and God will forgive your sins.' Many people . . . went out to hear John. They confessed their sins, and he baptized them in the River Jordan . . .

He announced . . . 'The man who will come after me is much greater than I am. I am not good enough even to bend down and untie his sandals. I baptize you with water, but he will baptize you with the Holy Spirit.'

John prepared the way for Jesus, so that when Jesus came the people were ready to listen to him.

Many people today aren't ready to listen to Jesus because they think that all Christians are hypocrites. But as we begin to serve people, like Michael did, we can help them to think again.

On the left are some people you might know who don't yet know Jesus. On the right are some ways in which you could serve them. Choose one of the people in the left hand column, and draw a line to link them with a way you could serve them.

An elderly relative	**Offer some baby-sitting***
Someone in your family	**Call in with the church mag**
A lonely neighbour	**Offer to do some gardening**
A single parent	**Offer some housework**
Someone recently bereaved	**Offer to do some shopping**

*Don't forget you need to be 14.

Lord Jesus, John the Baptist blazed the trail for you, and helped people to get ready to hear you. As I serve people around me, may my service blaze your trail too. Amen.

13

A group of Girl Guides from Halifax recently visited Mexico. They were shocked by what they saw there. They knew that many people in Mexico live poorer lives than in England. But nothing had quite prepared them for the reality of that.

Theirs, though, was a trip with a difference. They hadn't gone just to shake their heads and say 'that's awful'! They'd gone to make a difference.

During their visit, with the help of some volunteers, they built a house. It was just a simple wooden structure. But it was better than what went before. At least the family who live there now have a larger space to live in . . .and two windows

That group of teenage girls changed the world. They were living out the call of John the Baptist:

 *Read Luke 3:9–11*

'The axe is ready to cut down the trees at the roots; every tree that does not bear fruit will be cut down and thrown in the fire.'

The people asked him, 'What are we to do, then?'

He answered, 'Whoever has two shirts must give one to the man who has none, and whoever has food must share it.'

Change the world

John the Baptist was a fiery character. He burned with a passion to see God honoured. He knew that some had two shirts, others none. He hated that unfairness.

But like the Guides in Mexico, it didn't stop at words. John wanted God's servants to change the world—to do something positive for those in need.

In the left hand column, write things that you buy that you could do without.

In the middle column, write how much you could save if you didn't buy those things.

In the right hand column, make a note of people who could benefit from a gift of that money.

Dear Jesus, thank you for John the Baptist. He burned with anger at our unfair world. He wants me to change it. Give me the power of your Holy Spirit. Help me to change the world. Amen.

	£	

ONE PERSON DO?

Magnify Jesus

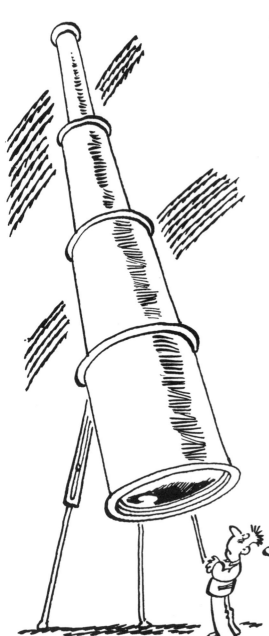

You can look two ways through a telescope. If you look through it the right way, the thing you're looking at gets bigger. If you look through it the wrong way, it gets smaller. Hold that in mind while I tell you about Sean and Robert . . .

Sean and Robert were both in their church worship group. Sean played drums; Robert the keyboard.

Sean loved being at the front. He loved people looking at him. He made a great show of his drumming, and made it very obvious he didn't like the 'boring old hymns'.

Robert wanted to fade into the background. He wanted people to worship God through his music. He didn't want to get in the way.

Sean is holding the telescope the wrong way round. He wants people to look at him . . . so Jesus fades into the background.

Robert's got the telescope the right way round. He fades into the background. Jesus is magnified.

John the Baptist had the telescope the right way too:

HOW COME THE MOON'S SO SMALL?

Read John 3:27–30

> *John answered, 'No one can have
> anything unless God gives it to him.
> You yourselves are my witnesses that
> I said, "I am not the Messiah, but I
> have been sent ahead of him." . . . He
> must become more important while I
> become less important.'*

Don't ever serve to get noticed, or to
show off. It's very tempting, but it's not
the way of Jesus.

Serve like John the Baptist did. Serve
so as to point to Jesus.

Hidden in the word square are ten ways
of serving. Try to find them all, and as
you find each one, put it in the 'Sean' or
'Robert' columns . . .

Sean	**Robert**
. . . .	. . . .
. . . .	. . . .
. . . .	. . . .
. . . .	. . . .
. . . .	. . . .

Loud
Public
Quiet
Boastful
Patient
Humble
Showing off
Private
Proud
Serving

```
L O U D R M N C T F
U E L B M U H T F R
F R F T J F P O M C
T H D M C R G R Z I
S E R V I N G S T L
A N L V I R F D E B
O P A W D E U L I U
B T O B T O T N U P
E H R S R B M R Q N
S B Y P A T I E N T
```

Now think about the way you serve
Jesus. Underline the word that best
describes your serving him.

*Lord Jesus, forgive me when the only
reason I serve you is to get noticed.
Like John the Baptist, help me to hold
the telescope the right way round.
May I become less important, and you
more important. Amen.*

15

Sarah was confused. Last week, at the big rally, it had seemed so right. There were lots of young people. The music was bright and uplifting; the speaker powerful and persuasive. She really had believed in God. She really had wanted to follow Jesus.

A week later it all seemed different. The fizz had gone out. It was raining and cold. Sarah wondered whether she'd imagined it all. She began to doubt whether God was really there.

Every Christian there's ever been has had 'highs' and 'lows'. Some days you could almost reach out and touch God. Other days you wonder if he's even there.

Don't be too hard on yourself on the 'downer' days. We all have them. Even John the Baptist, once he was in prison, began to doubt Jesus:

 *Read Luke 7:18–23*

> *John . . . called two of them and sent them to the Lord to ask him, 'Are you the one John said was going to come, or should we expect someone else?'*
>
> *When they came to Jesus, they said, 'John the Baptist sent us to ask if you are the one he said was going to come, or if we should expect someone else.'*
>
> *At that very time Jesus cured many people of their sicknesses, diseases, and evil spirits, and gave sight to many blind people. He answered John's messengers, 'Go back and tell John what you have seen and heard: the blind can see, the lame can walk . . . the dead are raised to life, and the Good News is preached to the poor. How happy are those who have no doubts about me!'*

When John the Baptist began to doubt him, Jesus pointed to all the wonderful things he was doing. He used things in the past to cheer John up in the present.

We can take a leaf out of Jesus' book. Think about the most recent time that God felt close. In the box below, jot down some notes of what happened.

```
Date: _____




```

Now write today's date on the line. And next time you're in the dumps, and wondering whether God's real, come back to your notes. Remind yourself of what he's done for you.

Was I right?

Lord Jesus, even John the Baptist doubted you. When you feel far away from me, help me not to get too depressed. Help me to remember the good things you've done for me. Amen.

16

In 1974, Janani Luwum became Archbishop of Uganda. Three years earlier, General Idi Amin had overthrown the legal government and become military dictator.

Amin began to wipe out everyone opposed to him. People of Asian birth were driven out of the country. People accused of false crimes were dragged out of their houses and shot.

Archbishop Luwum could not watch it happen. Publicly and privately, but always with great love, he rebuked Amin for his crimes.

Friends tried to persuade him to keep quiet, but Janani could not. He knew that to do so would be to deny Jesus. Eventually in 1977, he was arrested and shot dead.

Down the ages there have been Christians who have served Jesus all the way to death. John the Baptist was one of them. He was arrested and held in prison. One night a dancing girl so pleased King Herod that he offered her anything she wanted. She asked for John's head on a dish:

 Read Mark 6:26–29

This made the king very sad, but he could not refuse her because of the vows he had made . . . So he sent off a guard at once with orders to bring John's head. The guard left, went to the prison, and cut John's head off . . . When John's disciples heard about this, they came and took away his body, and buried it.

Janani Luwum and John the Baptist served Jesus no matter the cost. But here's the strange thing. In countries

All the

....AND I THOUGHT BEING A CHRISTIAN WAS AN EASY OPTION!!

where they have nothing to fear for their faith, Christians are often weak and limp in their following of Jesus.

So look at the statements below. Each of them describe Janani and John. Shade the bar to the extent that they describe you:

They were full of courage.

They followed Jesus with commitment.

They stood up for what is right.

They served without counting the cost.

Teach me, good Lord, to serve you as you deserve. To give and not to count the cost. To fight and not to heed the wounds. To toil and not to seek for rest. To labour and not to seek reward, save that of knowing that I do your will. Amen.

way to death

CHRISTIAN MARTYRS

'Why did I say I'd do it?!' Alix's heart was pounding. Her palms were clammy. Her stomach churned like a cement mixer.

It'd sounded such fun at the time—when the minister at Alix's church had first mentioned it. The idea was to act out some of Jesus' parables in the shopping precinct.

Now they were just about to go out, though, it all felt different. 'What if some friends from school see me? What if we get jeered at? What if I forget my lines?'

When the servant of Jesus is afraid, she needs to hear the words God spoke to Joseph. He was thinking of breaking his engagement to Mary:

 *Read Matthew 1:20–21*

While he was thinking about this, an angel of the Lord appeared to him in a dream and said, 'Joseph, descendant of David, do not be afraid to take Mary to be your wife. For it is by the Holy Spirit that she has conceived. She will have a son, and you will name him Jesus.'

'Joseph . . . do not be afraid . . . it is my will that you marry Mary and care for my Son Jesus.'

'Alix . . . do not be afraid . . . it is my will that you go out openly to speak of Jesus.'

If we really want to serve Jesus, we will sometimes find ourselves feeling afraid. After all, he will call us to do things we thought we couldn't do.

But when you're afraid, take some time to hear the words God spoke to Joseph. Jesus wants to speak them into your life too: 'Don't be afraid!'

SCRIPT

SHOPPING PRECINT THIS WAY—

Here are some ways you might need courage to serve Jesus. Which of them is he asking you to do? Put a tick in the left hand box.

☐ ☐ Read the lesson in church.
☐ ☐ Take part in street drama.
☐ ☐ Play an instrument in church.
☐ ☐ Speak about your faith at school.
☐ ☐ Invite a friend to church.
☐ ☐ Join the church drama group.

Now think about the jobs you ticked. Which of them are you afraid of? Put a tick in the right hand box.

Now choose something for which you gave two ticks. Write it in the space in this prayer:

Dear Jesus, I think you might be asking me to

. . . .

You know I'm afraid. Please fill me with courage—the courage that helped Joseph to serve you. Amen.

JOSEPH:
DON'T BE AFRAID

Brigadier Swann looked at his platoon. 'Right then, men. Wilson's been captured. We need some volunteers to rescue him.'

'Volunteers will swim through the shark-infested moat, climb the bank in full view of the searchlights, cut through the electric barbed wire, and rescue our man. Volunteers step forward a pace.'

There was a pause. Nobody moved. Then Corporal Cottee mumbled into his chest. 'Please sir, We don't want to do it. It sounds a bit dangerous.'

Brigadier Swann eyed his men with contempt. 'You shower!'

Throughout history, people have been called upon to do difficult and dangerous things. Things they'd rather not do. Some people, like Swann's platoon, shrink back.

But Mary didn't. God asked her to have a baby, before she was married, in a way that no one will ever fully understand. She answered the call:

 Read Luke 1:26–38

> *God sent the Angel Gabriel to . . . a young woman promised in marriage to a man named Joseph . . . Her name was Mary.*
>
> *The angel said to her, 'Don't be afraid, Mary; God has been gracious to you. You will become pregnant and give birth to a son, and you will name him Jesus . . .'*

MARY:

ANSWERING THE CALL

Mary said to the angel, 'I am a virgin. How, then, can this be?'

The angel answered, 'The Holy Spirit will come on you, and God's power will rest upon you. For this reason the holy child will be called the Son of God...'

'I am the Lord's servant,' said Mary; 'may it happen to me as you have said.'

If everyone said 'no' every time they were asked to do something difficult or dangerous, nothing of any value would ever get done.

That's why it's good to follow Mary's lead. God asked her to do something. She said 'yes'—*may it happen to me as you have said.*

So think about what Jesus is calling you to do. For each 'call', shade in the bar to the extent that you're willing to 'answer the call':

Jesus calls me to...

Give to the starving.

no	**yes**

Be quick to forgive.

no	**yes**

Accept all people, whatever their race.

no	**yes**

Pray for the sick.

no	**yes**

Live a life that honours God.

no	**yes**

Which 'call' have you shaded least? Write it in the space in the prayer.

Dear God, thank you for Mary. Thank you that she answered your call. Help me today to follow in her footsteps. Help me to

. . . .

Amen.

19 MARY:
DO WHATEVER HE TELLS YOU

The school party was deep inside the cave. Suddenly a boulder became dislodged. Water began pouring into the narrow passageway. What's worse, the lights fused and they were plunged into thick blackness.

There was panic. The water was up to their knees. People began to scream. Then the guide, Mr Johnston, switched on his helmet light. The panic began to die down.

'Right, children,' said their teacher, 'follow Mr Johnston. He knows these caves like the back of his hand. You'll be all right. Just do whatever he tells you . . .'

There would have been a moment of panic at the wedding we're about to read about. After all, the whole village was there, and the booze had run out.

But amid the panic was someone calm and level headed. It was Mary. She knew that Jesus was the way out of the trouble:

Read John 2:1–5

Two days later there was a wedding in the town of Cana in Galilee. Jesus' mother was there, and Jesus and his disciples had also been invited to the wedding. When the wine had given out, Jesus' mother said to him, 'They have no wine left.'

'You must not tell me what to do,' Jesus replied. 'My time has not yet come.'

Jesus' mother then told the servants, 'Do whatever he tells you.'

Mary knew that Jesus held the key. The servants did as he asked, and water was turned into wine. The party was rescued. Panic over!

She said *do whatever he tells you*, and her words have been very important for servants of Jesus. Like the guide leading the children out of the cave, Jesus only wants the best for us. So if we 'do whatever he tells us', then everything will work together for good.

The only thing is . . . how does Jesus 'tell us' what to do? Here's a list of ways he might use. Tick any that Jesus has used to speak to you:

- ☐ through a teacher
- ☐ through the words on a single/ album
- ☐ through the Bible
- ☐ through a television programme
- ☐ through my church youth group
- ☐ through sermons
- ☐ through worship songs
- ☐ through a film

Lord Jesus, thank you that you want only the best for me. You want to guide me right through my life. Help me to do whatever you tell me, and to learn to hear you speak. Amen.

'You've got to come with us! It's ace!' Paula had been to 'Laser Quest' for her birthday. It was the best thing ever. Now she was rounding up some friends so she could go again . . .

'You get these packs and these laser guns and it goes all dark and there's this loud music and you hide behind stuff and shoot each other. It's ace! Come with us!'

Whenever you discover something good, you want to tell your friends about it. You want them to have the experience that you've had.

That's just what Andrew did after he had met Jesus:

 Read John 1:35–42

. . . John was standing there . . . with two of his disciples, when he saw Jesus walking by. 'There is the Lamb of God!' he said.

The two disciples heard him say this and went with Jesus. Jesus turned, saw them following him, and asked, 'What are you looking for?'

They answered, 'Where do you live, Rabbi?' (This word means 'Teacher'.)

'Come and see,' he answered . . . So they went with him and saw where he lived, and spent the rest of that day with him.

One of them was Andrew, Simon Peter's brother. At once he found his brother Simon and told him, 'We have found the Messiah.' (This word means 'Christ'.) Then he took Simon to Jesus.

ANDREW: 20
BRING THEM TO JESUS!

Paula had a brilliant party at 'Laser Quest'. Of course she wanted her friends to join in.

Andrew met Jesus. He was convinced that Jesus was the one the world had been waiting for. So of course he went off to bring other people to meet him.

We're off to do the same today. We're servants of Jesus. We're convinced he's good news. And if he's good news, we want our friends to meet him too.

In the box, write the names of people among your friends who have not yet met Jesus:

Then, from this list, tick something to which you might invite your friends:
- ☐ Christian rock band
- ☐ Youth group weekend away
- ☐ Church service
- ☐ Christian club at school
- ☐ Church party
- ☐ Christian film/drama event

Lord Jesus, thank you for Andrew. Thank you that the first thing he did was to bring other people to meet you. I pray for my friends who don't yet know you. Help me to be like Andrew and to bring them to you. Amen.

IT'S ACE !!!

Have you ever noticed who wanted Jesus killed? It wasn't the Romans—they didn't really know who he was. It wasn't the crowds in Jerusalem—they were only stirred up by ringleaders.

It was the religious leaders. They wanted Jesus dead. He was on a collision course with them from the beginning. Time and again he showed them they were wrong. They were wrong about God. They were wrong about the Bible. They were wrong about what's important.

Among other things, Jesus clashed with the priests about 'who's out and who's in?'

For the priests, some people were very definitely 'in' (if they kept the hundreds of rules they were supposed to). But others were definitely 'out'—the lives they led meant the priests wanted nothing to do with them.

That's not the way of Jesus. Jesus is for all people. Just look what happens after he calls Matthew to follow him:

MATTHEW:
JESUS FOR ALL

Read Matthew 9:9–13

Jesus left that place, and as he walked along, he saw a tax collector, named Matthew, sitting in his office. He said to him, 'Follow me.'

Matthew got up and followed him.

While Jesus was having a meal in Matthew's house, many tax collectors and other outcasts came and joined Jesus and his disciples at the table. Some Pharisees saw this and asked his disciples, 'Why does your teacher eat with such people?'

Jesus heard them and answered, 'People who are well do not need a doctor, but only those who are sick . . . I have not come to call respectable people, but outcasts.'

For Jesus, no one is ever 'out'. No matter what they've done. No matter the colour of their skin. No matter how much or how little they've got—no one is ever 'out' with Jesus.

We who follow him should be the same. We serve all of humankind. It doesn't matter who they are or what they've done. If they're human, Jesus calls us to serve them.

Join these opposites with a line to show that all people matter to Jesus . . .

Young	Atheist
Christian	Healthy
Rich	Old
Sick	Woman
Man	Poor

Dear Jesus, thank you that you shocked 'religious' people. Thank you that you enjoyed eating with 'outcasts'. Thank you that all people matter to you. Amen.

Ian and Gavin were cycling along the canal towpath. Suddenly they saw a little girl struggling in the water. She obviously couldn't swim and would soon drown.

The boys dumped their bikes and dived in. They dragged her onto the tow-path and Gavin knelt to give her the kiss of life.

'Wait a minute!' cried Ian. 'I'm better at that than you. I've got my bronze life-saver's award.'

'So!' countered Gavin. 'I've got my Scouts First Aid badge and that's better!'

'Isn't!' shouted Ian. 'Is!' shouted Gavin, 'Isn't!' 'Is!' 'Isn't!' 'Is!' In the end they came to blows.

They were so busy fighting that they hardly noticed the experienced fell-walker. He came up behind them, gave the girl the kiss of life, and took her off to hospital.

It's a crazy story. And it wouldn't happen. But Jesus called twelve men to help him on a rescue mission. And two of them, James and John, once asked to be top dogs. The others were furious. It wasn't the only time Jesus' followers fell out:

Read Mark 9:33–35

> They came to Capernaum, and . . . Jesus asked his disciples, 'What were you arguing about on the road?'
> But they would not answer him, because on the road they had been arguing among themselves about who was the greatest. Jesus sat down, called the twelve disciples, and said to them, 'Whoever wants to be the first must place himself last of all and be the servant of all.'

HANG ON!! WE'LL RESCUE YOU AS SOON AS WE'VE AGREED WHO'S THE BEST SWIMMER!!

JAMES AND JOHN:
WHO'S THE GREATEST?

Ian and Gavin's story is a bit like the story of the Church. Jesus wants the Church to rescue the world. We spend too much time fighting each other.

So, servant of Jesus, hear his call: 'If you want to be first in my kingdom, place yourself last and be the servant of all.'

Here are five reasons why it's sad when followers of Jesus fight each other. Score each of them out of 10 for the impact they make on you:

It's sad when Christians fight, because...

We waste energy we could be using to serve the world.

1   2   3   4   5   6   7   8   9   10

Jesus commanded us to love one another.

1   2   3   4   5   6   7   8   9   10

We put other people off finding out about Jesus.

1   2   3   4   5   6   7   8   9   10

We hurt each other.

1   2   3   4   5   6   7   8   9   10

We sometimes cause people to leave the Church.

1   2   3   4   5   6   7   8   9   10

Dear Jesus, like you I'm sad when your followers argue with each other. Help us to live at peace with each other. And help me to play my part in being a peacemaker. Amen.

Mrs Collins sighed deeply. She had a thumping headache, and was only half way through the pile of ironing. In the living room, the twins were fighting. Mrs Collins looked at the clock and hoped that Clare would soon be home.

Clare had been away for the weekend with the Youth Fellowship. At last, at quarter past six, Mrs Collins heard the front door. Clare was back.

'Hi Mum!' she said, as she dumped a bag of dirty washing on the floor. 'It's been great! Fiona got blessed in the Spirit, and Samantha's boyfriend became a Christian! Mum, you should spend more time with God, you look really run down. Anyway, I'll tell you about it later: we've got Praise Fellowship at half six. Bye!'

Housework . . . or time with Jesus. That was the issue when Jesus met two sisters:

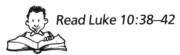 **Read Luke 10:38–42**

. . . Jesus . . . came to a village where . . . Martha welcomed him in her home. She had a sister named Mary, who sat down at the feet of the Lord and listened to his teaching. Martha was upset over all the work she had to do, so she came and said, 'Lord, don't you care that my sister has left me to do all the work by myself? Tell her to come and help me!'

The Lord answered her, 'Martha, Martha! You are worried and troubled over so many things, but just one is needed. Mary has chosen the right thing, and it will not be taken away from her.'

Martha was busy with the housework. Mary chose to sit at Jesus' feet. Jesus said that Mary had made the better choice.

But there are some people who cannot make that choice. A single mum, like Mrs Collins, may have so much to do that she has little time to spend with God. Clare could have offered to baby-sit the twins so her Mum could go to the evening service.

So have a think. Who do you know who's so busy they can't spend enough time with God? Write their name in the top of the box:

In the bottom, jot down something you would do to help them, so that they can spend some 'Mary time' with God.

Dear Jesus, help me to notice when people around me have too much to do. Help me to do all I can to lighten their load. Amen.

MARTHA AND MARY:
THE HOUSEWORK FACTOR

24

Mary was crushed. She'd believed so much in Jesus. She really had believed that he was the one. He'd promised them so much. Then, they'd watched him die: a cruel, unfair death. They'd even let a murderer free in his place.

Now, standing by his tomb, she couldn't get her mind round what was happening. She'd come to visit his grave, and it was empty.

As she stood, looking into that black hole, trying to piece it all together, she suddenly heard a voice behind her. It called her name:

 Read John 20:16–17

Jesus said to her, 'Mary!'

She turned towards him and said in Hebrew, 'Rabboni!' (This means 'Teacher'.)

'Do not hold on to me,' Jesus told her, 'because I have not yet gone back up to the Father. But go to my brothers and tell them that I am returning to him who is my Father and their Father, my God and their God.'

Mary had been looking into a black hole. It summed up all her crushed hopes. Then Jesus called her name. She turned round . . . and saw Jesus standing there.

Let's call that 'Mary's turn'. It's a turn from darkness to light, from despair to hope, from fear to faith.

Now think about what 'Mary's turn' might mean for you.

If you decide to spend your whole life serving Jesus, there will be times when you'll face disappointment. Something you'd hoped for might crumble. You're left looking into a black hole.

If that ever happens, don't forget the rest of the story. For Jesus will want to call you by name. He'll want to turn you round from despair to faith. He'll want to strengthen you, with his life in yours. He'll want to assure you that in the kingdom of God, all is never lost.

Unscramble the letters to find five versions of 'Mary's turn':

Make me a channel of your peace. Where there is hatred let me bring your love; Where there is injury, your pardon, Lord; And where there's doubt, true faith in you. Amen.

From SNERDAKS .... **to THLIG** ....

From RIPSEAD .... **to EPHO** ....

From AREF .... **to THIAF** ....

From THREAD .... **to VLOE** ....

From WASKSNEE .... **to WROPE** ....

25

Debbie's car sped through the traffic. A lorry had crashed, and she was off to cover the incident for the local paper.

She reached the scene and asked a passer-by what had happened: 'I'd just got off the bus when this lorry careered down the hill. He swerved to avoid the crossing and ploughed into that flower-bed. I'm so pleased he's not seriously hurt.'

If something's happened while you're somewhere else the only thing you can do is talk to witnesses. That's what journalists do all the time. Without eye-witnesses there'd be no story.

Jesus' first followers had a story. They'd seen Jesus die. They'd met him alive. But at first Thomas didn't believe them:

 **Read John 20:25–28**

... Thomas said to them, 'Unless I see the scars of the nails in his hands and put my finger on those scars and my hand in his side, I will not believe.'

A week later the disciples were together again indoors, and Thomas was with them. The doors were locked, but Jesus came and stood among them and said, 'Peace be with you.' Then he said to Thomas, 'Put your finger here, and look at my hands; then stretch out your hand and put it in my side. Stop your doubting, and believe!'

Thomas answered him, 'My Lord and my God!'

At first Thomas would not believe the eye-witnesses. But he was open to being persuaded. And when he met the risen Jesus he *was* persuaded: *My Lord and my God!*

We live two thousand years later. But we still have the eye-witness accounts. Like Thomas, we must be honest if we can't bring ourselves to believe them yet. But, like Thomas, we must also be open to being persuaded. And ready to say to Jesus: *My Lord and my God!*

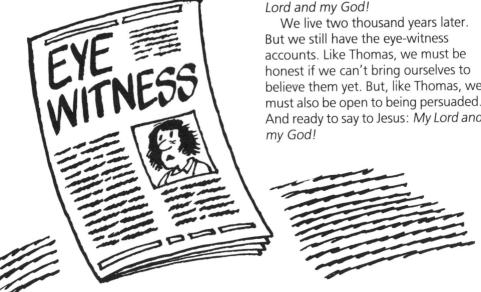

THOMAS:
BELIEVE THE WITNESSES

Here are some things the eye-witnesses tell us about Jesus. Are there any you find hard to believe? If so, underline them, and then talk them through with your youth leader:

He was born in a stable.

He was often followed by huge crowds.

He healed sick people.

He fed 5,000 people with five loaves and two fish.

He died after being nailed to a cross.

Three days after he died his followers met him alive.

Lord Jesus, thank you for the eye-witness accounts of your life. Help me to be honest about my doubts—but ready to call you 'Lord'. Amen.

26 STEPHEN:
STAND UP FOR WHAT'S RIGHT

As Hitler's grip on Germany grew stronger, a tide of evil swept across his country. People were no longer free to express their opinion. If they opposed the Nazis it meant imprisonment or death. You couldn't even send a letter without the fear of it being opened.

Worse followed. All people of Jewish descent were labelled 'impure'. Eventually the concentration camps started the grim task of executing Jews in their millions.

Sadly, many Church leaders said nothing. But not Dietrich Bonhoeffer. He was a German pastor who stood up for what is right. He bitterly opposed what the Nazis were doing. Eventually he was arrested. Shortly before the end of the Second World War he was hanged.

It's never been easy to make a stand. If people around us are doing wrong, it's much easier to go with the flow.

That's not an option for God's servants. Here's one of them, Stephen, standing up for Jesus against the very people who murdered him:

 Read Acts 7:51–58

'How stubborn you are!' Stephen went on to say. 'How . . . deaf you are to God's message! You are just like your ancestors: you too have always resisted the Holy Spirit! Was there any prophet that your ancestors did not persecute? They killed God's messengers, who long ago announced the coming of his righteous Servant. And now you have betrayed and murdered him . . .'

As the members of the Council listened to Stephen, they became furious . . .

Then they all rushed at him at once, threw him out of the city, and stoned him.

Both Stephen and Dietrich Bonhoeffer stood up for what is right. They both paid a high price. But they stood firm for Jesus.

Let's do the same. However hard it may be at times, let's stand against evil, wherever we find it. Let's stand up for all that's good.

Shade in each bar to the extent you match the description:

I never look down on someone of a different race.

If people are picking on someone I never side with the bullies.

If people make jokes about God I don't join in.

When people tease me for going to church it doesn't put me off.

Lord Jesus, make me strong. Help me to stand up for you, and for all that's right. Amen.

JUST BECAUSE YOU ARE ALL GOING THAT WAY DOESN'T MAKE IT RIGHT!

Mick was always in trouble with the police. If it wasn't drugs it was theft. If it wasn't theft it was beating people up.

Mick's wife, Ros, was a Christian. But even though Mick could see that her friends 'had something', he didn't want to find out what it was.

Then something happened. Mick met Jesus for himself. He went to see Ros' vicar 'to have a go at him'. But as they talked, the penny dropped. God was for real. He was calling Mick to follow him.

That was ten years ago. Today, Mick works for the Church Army on an estate in Barnsley. He goes out befriending the teenagers who hang around the streets. He tells them about his past, and tries to guide them away from drugs and burglary. He's taken groups of them camping, and into prisons—to show them it's not the doss they sometimes think.

Mick is living proof of something very important about serving Jesus: it doesn't matter what's in your past. Whatever you've done, he'll never write you off.

That's what Saint Paul discovered. To begin with, he did all he could to stamp out faith in Jesus. Then something happened:

Read Acts 26:13–18

'. . .I saw a light much brighter than the sun, coming from the sky and shining round me . . . I heard a voice say to me in Hebrew, "Saul, Saul! Why are you persecuting me?" . . . "Who are you, Lord?" I asked. And the Lord answered, "I am Jesus, whom you persecute. But get up and stand on your feet. I have appeared to you to appoint you as my servant. You are to tell others what you have seen of me today . . . You are to open their eyes and turn them from the darkness to the light . . . so that through their faith in me they will have their sins forgiven and receive their place among God's chosen people." '

Now pray:

Lord Jesus, thank you that you never write me off. Please forgive what's in my past. And help me to serve you in the future. Amen.

It doesn't matter what's in your past. Jesus is more interested in your future. That's what Paul discovered. It's what Mick discovered. It can be true for you, too.

Now rub out what you wrote in the box. Jesus has forgiven you!

Repeat the exercise from unit 7. In the box, lightly in pencil, write some of the things you'd like Jesus to forgive you for:

PAUL:
BEFORE AND AFTER

PAUL:
LIVING IT OUT

Everyone waited with bated breath for the final figure. 'And the final total raised was . . . Five . . . thousand . . . pounds!' The church burst into cheering and applause.

The church's teenagers had raised the money. They'd taken over an empty shop in town and opened a 'Christmas Cracker Restaurant', where everyone pays over the odds for the food they order.

Now they celebrated the results of their work: five thousand pounds. But not a penny of it was for them. The money went on clean water projects for the Third World.

God's servants are like that. Other people come first. They'd said they wanted to follow Jesus. Now they were living it out.

As they did, they were following in the footsteps of Saint Paul. He became aware of some very needy people, and organized a special collection for them. Here's how he urged his readers to give:

 Read 2 Corinthians 9:7–13

> *You should each give, then, as you have decided, not with regret or out of a sense of duty; for God loves the one who gives gladly. And God . . . will always make you rich enough to be generous at all times, so that many will thank God for your gifts which they receive from us. For this service you perform not only meets the needs of God's people, but also produces an outpouring of gratitude to God. And because of the proof which this service of yours brings, many will give glory to God for your loyalty to the gospel of Christ . . . and for your generosity in sharing with them and everyone else.*

Both our church's teenagers, and Paul's readers, were 'living it out'. They believed in God. They wanted to follow Jesus. They wanted to make life better for other people.

So have a think what you might do. Here's a list of ideas:

Spend a couple of Saturdays washing neighbours' cars for £2 a time and give all the money to Christian Aid (PO Box 100, London, SE1 7RT).

Once every two months for a whole year give away one week's pocket money to the Leprosy Mission (50 Portland Place, London, W1 3DG).

Write to Christmas Cracker (5 Ethel Street, Birmingham, B2 4BG) and ask about their latest projects.

Lord Jesus, you told us we'd always have the poor with us. Help me to do all I can to help them. Amen.

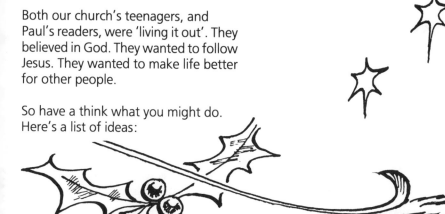

Barnabas: the encourager

Listen in to these two football teams. Which one do you think will play better?

First the blue team: 'Oh, Darren! Wasted pass again!' 'What are you doing in goal? You're useless!' 'That was your fault, four-eyes!'

And secondly, the reds: 'Never mind, Graham—good effort!' 'Great ball, Tony!' 'Well done—you're playing better all the time!'

I know which team I'd rather play for. I'd rather play for the reds. They're all encouraging each other. They'll stand a far better chance.

Any team needs encouragers— people who'll use words to build the others up. That's how Barnabas got his name, and why Barnabas was such a special part of Paul's team:

 Read Acts 4:36–37

> And so it was that Joseph, a Levite born in Cyprus, whom the apostles called Barnabas (which means 'One who Encourages'), sold a field he owned, brought the money, and handed it over to the apostles.

Like any football team, the church needs encouragers. It's so easy to run people down. It's very hurtful too. But it costs nothing to use a few words to build someone up.

So be a 'Barnabas' in your church. Get known as someone who encourages people.

Who do you know who could do with some encouragement? Write their names in the top box:

Lord Jesus, make me a Barnabas. May I be known as 'One who Encourages'. Amen.

In the second box, write what you will say to them.

BLUES!! — YOU'RE A WASTE OF SPACE!!

In the third box, make a note of when and how you'll say it.

30

Michelle had just started a paper round. The door of one of the houses was ajar when she got there. As she pushed the paper through she heard a voice inside, calling to her.

It turned out that a lonely old lady lived in that house. She hardly had any visitors. She'd watched the vicar going by, but he'd never called.

As soon as Michelle met the old lady, she set to work. She went out and got some shopping. She popped back later with some flowers. She called in to see the vicar to let him know of the old lady's plight.

True servants of Jesus are generous people. Not just with their money. With their time as well. They show the love of God in action.

That's just what Lydia did. Lydia was the first person in Europe to believe in Jesus. She showed the same generous spirit as Michelle:

 Read Acts 16:13–15

> *On the Sabbath we went out of the city to the riverside, where we thought there would be a place where Jews gathered for prayer. We sat down and talked to the women who gathered there. One of those who heard us was Lydia from Thyatira, who was a dealer in purple cloth. She was a woman who worshipped God, and the Lord opened her mind to pay attention to what Paul was saying. After she and the people of her house had been baptized, she invited us, 'Come and stay in my house if you have decided that I am a true believer in the Lord.' And she persuaded us to go.*

See? Lydia believed in Jesus. She generously put her faith into action. She opened her home to Paul and the others. She was generous for Jesus.

We can be like Lydia. We can be like Michelle. We can ask God to make us generous people, who live out his love in lives of practical service.

Are you 'generous for Jesus'? Score yourself out of 10 for the following:

Lydia: generous for Jesus

I'm happy to give what money I have to the poor.

1 2 3 4 5 6 7 8 9 10

I'm quick to lend people things if they ask to borrow them.

1 2 3 4 5 6 7 8 9 10

I love buying presents for people.

1 2 3 4 5 6 7 8 9 10

I'm willing to use my time to look after people who need help.

1 2 3 4 5 6 7 8 9 10

I go beyond what's expected of me in serving people.

1 2 3 4 5 6 7 8 9 10

Heavenly Father, by your Holy Spirit, make me generous for Jesus. Amen.

31

ER... GERBIL?...
RAT?... ER... RABBIT?
ER... MOUSE?... ER...
FERRET?

Gavin wanted the stage to open up and swallow him. He'd forgotten his lines yet again. From the wings came the hissed prompt from the drama teacher: 'Don't eat that . . . that's my hamster!'

'Don't eat that . . . that's my hamster!' Gavin repeated. People laughed politely but Gavin was burning with embarrassment. At the end he changed slowly, hoping that everyone would have left by the time he'd finished.

They hadn't. Sat waiting for him at the foot of the stairs was Paul, his best friend. He was just who Gavin wanted to see. 'Come on,' said Paul. 'Let's go swimming.'

Half an hour later, they were in the pool. But Gavin couldn't get his mind off the play. What a disaster! He stood by the poolside and winced.

Luke: faithful friend

Then, suddenly, he heard Paul running up behind him. 'Don't worry about it!' cried Paul, and he pushed Gavin into the deep end.

There are times when things get really difficult. Something goes wrong and you're embarrassed, or afraid. What you need then is friends. Friends who'll stick by you whatever.

Saint Paul had a friend like that. He was called Luke:

 Read 2 Timothy 4:9–11

Do your best to come to me soon. Demas fell in love with this present world and has deserted me, going off to Thessalonica. Crescens went to Galatia, and Titus to Dalmatia. Only Luke is with me.

Saint Paul often faced difficulties. But among the hardest would have been people like Demas, Crescens and Titus leaving him in the lurch. Once they'd worked so closely with him. When things had got tough, they'd sloped off.

That's why it would have been all the more important to have a friend like Luke: one who stood by him, even when everyone else left you to it.

We need to follow Luke's example. If we're serious about serving Jesus we need to stick by our friends, whatever happens.

In the box, write the names of your best friends:

Now pray . . .

Lord Jesus, thank you that Luke was a faithful friend to Paul. Help me to be like him. Help me to stick by my friends through thick and thin.
Amen.

What next?

The *Following Jesus* Series

If you have enjoyed using *Serving Jesus*, you might like to look at other titles in the series. All are available singly or in packs of 10 copies.

Following Jesus—31 units which explore the basics of the Christian faith.

Praying with Jesus—31 units which explore Jesus' teaching on prayer.

The Power of Jesus—28 units which consider the power of Jesus as seen in the seven signs in John's Gospel.

Picturing Jesus—28 units which consider the seven 'I Am' sayings in John's Gospel—the pictures which Jesus used to illustrate and show who he was: 'I am the Good Shepherd', 'I am the Vine', 'I am the Bread of Life', 'I am the Way, the Truth and the Life', 'I am the Light of the World', 'I am the Resurrection and the Life', 'I am the Gate'.

Stories by Jesus—31 units which consider ways Jesus used parables to illustrate his teaching and shows how they still relate to and challenge us 2,000 years later.

Surprised by Jesus—31 units which consider ways in which Jesus surprised people by what he said and what he did.

The Spirit of Jesus—31 units which consider the Holy Spirit: the story of the Spirit, pictures of the Spirit and the Holy Spirit and you.

The Teaching of Jesus—29 units consider the teaching of Jesus in the Sermon on the Mount (Matthew 5–7).

Sent by Jesus—30 units which show how Paul, the former enemy of Jesus, became his biggest fan.

The Touch of Jesus—28 units which look at the impact of the transforming touch of Jesus on those he met.

The final volume in the series, *The Cross of Jesus*, is in preparation.

All titles in the series are illustrated throughout by Taffy, and are available now from all good Christian bookshops, or in case of difficulty from BRF, Peter's Way, Sandy Lane West, Oxford, OX4 5HG.

If you would like to know more about the full range of Bible reading notes and other Bible reading group study materials published by BRF, write and ask for a free catalogue.